THE
JOURNAL
PR*JECT

MY SENIOR YEAR THROUGH MOM'S EYES

The Journal Project: My Senior Year Through Mom's Eyes
Copyright© 2023 by Cindy Manko

Library of Congress Cataloging-in-Publication Data

Library of Congress Number: 2023912323 | ISBN: 978-1-961732-08-7 (paperback) | ISBN: 978-1-961732-09-4 (print)

Published in association with Called Creatives Publishing, www.calledcreativespublishing.com

Cover design: Called Creatives Publishing
Interior design: Cindy Manko and Lori Block

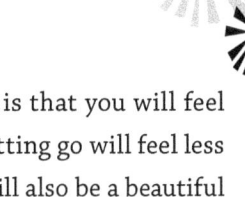

DEAR MOM,

I am so glad you chose this journal! My promise is that you will feel closer than ever to your high school senior, and letting go will feel less like losing them after completing this journal. It will also be a beautiful keepsake to give to your high school senior at the end of the school year. They will cherish the words you have for them.

This journal is also a gift to you. As you write to your child, you will be reminded of all that you have taught them. It will help you let go while drawing you closer than ever to your child.

"I write because I don't know what I think until I read what I say."
—Flannery O'Connor

When I wrote a journal to my children throughout their senior years, I had no idea how the process would benefit ME. And as this quote suggests, I didn't know what I knew until I wrote in those journals. I knew it would be fun for them to read about the details of their senior years, but it also revealed life lessons and a deep connection to my children during that uncertain time of letting go.

The writing reminded me of how far they had come. I was reminded of their strengths and abilities. It helped me process what they were experiencing in a deeper way which led to conversations that connected us deeper emotionally. In a time when the world says to disconnect, I was processing the fruits of my labor as a mom, seeing all that was created in my children as a result of parenting them for 18 years. I saw it plain as day; it was OK to let go. They were ready!

You are probably in awe at how the years have flown by. Even more reason to use this time to process what has been and will be. You could choose to let the year go by, being a bystander and only catching glimpses of time to express your love and share your heart with your very busy child. Or you can spend some quality time with this journal, sharing your most cherished memories, pondering the gifts of your grown and ready-to-fly child, and soaking in how far they have come.

<u>Things to remember when filling out this journal</u>:

- You do not have to be a writer to journal to your senior successfully. No one is grading your work. Your child will read it, hearing your voice, so write exactly what you want to say. It is that simple.

- Not all journal prompts will pertain to you and your child. Share an opinion anyway. Our children love to know what we think about things.

- Sometimes, the prompts will feel heavy and tough to process. I suggest having a blank journal for yourself to use to process. Pay close attention to big feelings. Emotions warn us about things around us.

  Addressing big feelings/emotions is one of the most important skills we can model for our high school seniors. Help them with this and write about it as a reminder lesson. Getting it just right can be a game changer with sensitive topics. Guard your tender heart (and your child's) and give yourself time.

- Although I have given many prompts to help you pull out important lessons and give encouragement, I have provided space to write messages specific to your child that have happened throughout each month in the *Monthly Notes and Letter* section in the back of this book. This is where day-to-day items can be written. I.e., "Today you sent in your college application, and I couldn't be prouder of you." Or "Today you experienced hate from _____, and that hurt me as much as it did you." Single statements like these are good, but what's better is your thoughts and advice in these situations. Do not be afraid to expound on how something affected both of you in the *Monthly Letters*. Talk about what you saw in the moment and all the things you know about your child that helped them persevere. When they read about how they persevered, it will be a great encouragement to them and will give them confidence in similar situations in the future.

- You will revisit topics. For example, a new boyfriend/girlfriend might be exciting and sweet initially but later be another heartbreak. Ongoing conversations will come up throughout the year. Connect those lessons for your child in the *Monthly Letters*. Consistent support and love in the ups and downs throughout the year will shine when they read all that happened and how you invested your whole being in helping them through it all.

QR Code: Just for you, Mom!

I have created a separate resource just for you as you write in this journal. This content is full of tips to help you communicate and connect with your high school senior. It will give you some remarkable things to write about. Not only have I successfully (not always gracefully) raised three kids through those teen years, but I have also done a deep dive into the science and psychology of raising a teen.

There is no finger-pointing in this content; rather, it encourages conversations with your teen while also providing pressure-releasing techniques as you parent through their senior year. My intention is to lead you through a successful, joy-filled year. When you scan this QR code, you will find:

- Chapter reviews with more suggestions and encouragement and sample journal entries.

- Parent tips for surviving the tough stuff throughout the year.

- Important information regarding college-bound kids as well as information supporting those choosing other routes.

- Science and psychology-backed approaches to talking to your senior.
- Creative ideas for homecoming, prom, grad party, and more!

<u>First things first</u>: Write your opening letter.

Here are some prompts to help you write your opening letter on page 1. You can find an example of an opening letter in the QR code content.

- As you anticipate an outstanding senior year, I anticipate the same. I get so emotional about:
- I am looking forward to:
- Big decisions you will make:
- These are my favorite ways to connect with you:
- I am so proud of you for:
- I love you (yes, just I love you! Write it, say it, repeat it!)

DEAR _____,

You are among the luckiest high school graduates because you have a mom who cares so deeply for you that she has completed her own senior project this year: this journal. The work she has invested in you to build memories and give you space to grow is commendable. Not all moms do this special kind of work for their children. It took a lot of "hard" work and a lot of "heart" work.

It was **HARD WORK** for her to complete this book.
It was ***HEART* WORK** writing about how much she loves you.

It was **HARD WORK** for her to watch you go through challenging moments this year.
It was **HEART WORK** being there for you unconditionally.

It was **HARD WORK** cooking, cleaning, and helping you have a smoother schedule.
It was **HEART WORK** handing over some responsibilities to you.

It was **HARD WORK** setting new boundaries to accommodate your growing independence.
It was **HEART WORK** loving you through your mistakes and insecurities.

It was **HARD WORK** keeping worry at bay.
It was **HEART WORK** reminding herself how capable you are.

It was **HARD WORK** finding time with you throughout the year.
It was **HEART WORK** letting you spend so much time with your friends.

It was **HARD WORK** holding back tears watching you prepare for your future.
It was **HEART WORK** letting you go because your independence depended on it!

Congratulations on your new launch into the next phase of your life, whatever that looks like. May all the lasting lessons your mom taught you carry you through. And may the most important lesson be that you have a mom with a heart of gold who will always be that voice of reason, steady support, and warm vote of confidence when you need it. She believes in you more than you'll ever know.

Best regards,
Cindy Manko, Author

THE JOURNAL PR❋JECT

Table of Contents

The date this journal was started ___/___/_____

Opening Letter

Date: ___ / ___ / _____

DEAR _____,

_____

_____

_____

_____

_____

_____

_____

_____

_____

_____

_____

_____

_____

_____

_____

_____

_____

_____

_____

_____

_____

_____

_____

_____

OPENING LETTER

CHAPTER 1

A WALK DOWN MEMORY LANE

Full name:

_____

Birth date:

_____

Why we named you this:

_____

_____

Nickname(s):

_____

These people share your birthday (google who was born on your child's birthdate):

_____

_____

Birthplace:

_____

This is what I remember about the day you were born:

_____

_____

_____

_____

_____

This is what surprised me the most in the first moments as your mom:

_____

_____

_____

_____

When you were little, you always _____

_____

_____

When I think of your childhood birthdays and holidays, this is what I think of:

_____

_____

_____

_____

Here are a few toddler memories that stand out:

_____

_____

_____

_____

_____

_____

_____

_____

_____

_____

The Bookends of School

Your first day of kindergarten went like this:

_____

_____

_____

_____

The first day of your senior year went like this:

_____

_____

_____

_____

When you were little, you always wanted to be

(profession) _____.

NOW, you aspire to be _____.

No matter what you decide to do as a profession, never stop being you.
These are the things that make you a spectacular human:

_____

_____

_____

_____

_____

_____

_____

Kindergarten
School Picture

Senior
Picture

Elementary School

These are some of my favorite memories of you in elementary school:

_____

_____

_____

_____

_____

_____

_____

_____

_____

_____

_____

_____

_____

_____

You were involved in these activities:

_____

_____

_____

_____

_____

_____

_____

Your favorite thing to wear was:

_____

_____

Your friends, family, teachers, or mentors that you were closest to:

_____

_____

_____

_____

_____

_____

You learned these life lessons:

_____

_____

_____

_____

_____

_____

This is what I remember most about being your mom at this stage of your life:

_____

_____

_____

_____

_____

_____

Middle School

These are some of my favorite memories of you in middle school:

_____

_____

_____

_____

_____

_____

_____

_____

_____

_____

_____

_____

_____

_____

_____

_____

You were involved in these activities:

_____

_____

_____

_____

_____

Your favorite thing to wear was:

_____

_____

Your friends, family, teachers, or mentors that you were closest to:

_____

_____

_____

_____

_____

_____

You learned these life lessons:

_____

_____

_____

_____

_____

_____

This is what I remember most about being your mom at this stage of your life:

_____

_____

_____

_____

_____

_____

High School

These are some of my favorite memories of you in high school:

_____

_____

_____

_____

_____

_____

_____

_____

_____

_____

_____

_____

_____

_____

_____

_____

You were involved in these activities:

_____

_____

_____

_____

_____

_____

_____

Your favorite thing to wear was:

_____

_____

Your friends, family, teachers, or mentors that you were closest to:

_____

_____

_____

_____

_____

_____

You learned these life lessons:

_____

_____

_____

_____

_____

_____

This is what I remember most about being your mom at this stage of your life:

_____

_____

_____

_____

_____

Other memories and thoughts:

_____
_____
_____
_____
_____
_____
_____
_____
_____
_____
_____
_____
_____
_____
_____
_____
_____
_____
_____
_____
_____
_____

CHAPTER 2

I NOTICE

I notice your eyes light up when:

_____

_____

_____

_____

_____

_____

_____

I notice you get sad when:

_____

_____

_____

_____

_____

_____

_____

I notice you struggle when:

_____

_____

_____

_____

_____

_____

_____

I notice you are energized when:

_____

_____

_____

_____

_____

_____

_____

I notice you're most productive when:

_____

_____

_____

_____

_____

_____

_____

I notice you are most yourself when you are with:

_____

_____

_____

_____

_____

_____

_____

Things people notice about you:

_____

_____

_____

_____

_____

_____

_____

You are unique in this way:

_____

_____

_____

_____

_____

_____

_____

I am curious to know this about you:

_____

_____

_____

_____

_____

_____

_____

CHAPTER 3

YOU ARE VALUABLE

The personality traits that make you amazing are:

_____

_____

_____

_____

_____

_____

_____

_____

_____

_____

While I have complete confidence in you, I have seen you question yourself when:

_____

_____

_____

_____

_____

_____

_____

_____

_____

_____

_____

So many people see the value in you. I get compliments all the time. The nicest compliment I have received about you is:

_____

_____

_____

_____

_____

_____

_____

This is my favorite thing about being your mom:

_____

_____

_____

_____

_____

_____

_____

This is the way you have made me a better person:

_____

_____

_____

_____

_____

_____

CHAPTER 4

EVERY MOM
HAS TO SAY
THESE THINGS

This is why I say what I say:

"I love you"

_____

_____

_____

_____

"Be careful"

_____

_____

_____

_____

"Think before you act"

_____

_____

_____

_____

"Be helpful"

_____

_____

_____

_____

"Do your best"

_____
_____
_____
_____
_____
_____
_____

"Be a good friend"

_____
_____
_____
_____
_____
_____
_____

Others...

_____
_____
_____
_____
_____
_____
_____

CHAPTER 5

PASSIONS
AND INTERESTS

(Sports, Robotics, The Arts, Music…)

These are your talents and strengths:

_____

_____

_____

_____

_____

_____

_____

_____

_____

_____

_____

_____

_____

_____

The hobbies, clubs, and sports you are a part of:

_____

_____

_____

_____

_____

_____

_____

_____

_____

_____

_____

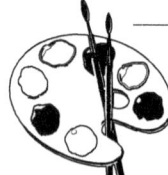 _____

_____

Your favorite hobby/sport/activity and why:

_____

_____

_____

_____

_____

_____

_____

Everyone has a role on a team. These are the roles you play in your activities:

_____

_____

_____

_____

_____

_____

_____

I am so proud of you for:

_____

_____

_____

_____

_____

_____

_____

The most exciting moment was:

_____

_____

_____

_____

_____

_____

_____

The biggest disappointment was:

_____

_____

_____

_____

_____

_____

_____

The obstacles you overcame were:

_____

_____

_____

_____

_____

_____

_____

I will miss:

_____

_____

_____

_____

_____

_____

Personal accomplishments and awards:

_____

_____

_____

_____

_____

_____

_____

These are the coaches or mentors that had a significant impact on you:

_____

_____

_____

_____

_____

_____

_____

More details about your extracurricular activities.

_____

_____

_____

_____

_____

_____

_____

_____

_____

_____

_____

_____

_____

_____

_____

_____

_____

_____

_____

_____

_____

_____

_____

_____

_____

_____

_____

_____

More details about your extracurricular activities.

_____

_____

_____

_____

_____

_____

_____

_____

_____

_____

_____

_____

_____

_____

_____

_____

_____

_____

_____

_____

_____

_____

_____

_____

_____

_____

_____

_____

_____

_____

PASSIONS AND INTERESTS

More details about your extracurricular activities.

_____
_____
_____
_____
_____
_____
_____
_____
_____
_____
_____
_____
_____
_____
_____
_____
_____
_____
_____
_____
_____
_____
_____
_____
_____

CHAPTER 6

FAMILY

About our family:

_____

_____

_____

_____

_____

_____

_____

_____

_____

_____

_____

Family values (beliefs, ethics, priorities, and worldviews):

_____

_____

_____

_____

_____

_____

_____

_____

_____

_____

_____

_____

Family traditions:

_____

_____

_____

_____

_____

_____

_____

_____

_____

_____

_____

Your relationship with your siblings:

_____

_____

_____

_____

_____

_____

_____

_____

_____

_____

_____

FAMILY

Family pets:

_____

_____

_____

_____

_____

Extended family:

_____

_____

_____

_____

_____

_____

_____

Favorite family vacation and why:

_____

_____

_____

_____

_____

_____

_____

_____

_____

CHAPTER 7

SOCIAL LIFE

Cell Phones

You were _____ years old when you got your first cell phone.

I was _____ years old when I got my first cell phone.

Things I love about cell phones:

_____

_____

_____

_____

Things I dislike about cell phones:

_____

_____

_____

_____

Social Media

Things I love about social media:

_____

_____

_____

_____

Things I dislike about social media:

_____

_____

_____

_____

Using the Car

Things I love about you being able to drive:

_____

_____

_____

_____

Things I dislike about you being able to drive:

_____

_____

_____

_____

Choosing Relationships

These are the friends you've been hanging out with this year:

_____

_____

_____

_____

_____

Your favorite places to hangout:

_____

_____

_____

_____

_____

This is the impact your friendships have had on you:

_____

_____

_____

_____

_____

This is what true friendship means to me:

_____

_____

_____

This is what makes you a good friend:

_____
_____
_____
_____
_____

My thoughts on dating:

_____
_____
_____
_____
_____

How you should be treated in a relationship:

_____
_____
_____
_____
_____

This is what true love is:

_____
_____
_____
_____
_____

CHAPTER 8

DEALING WITH PAIN, PANIC, AND PRESSURE

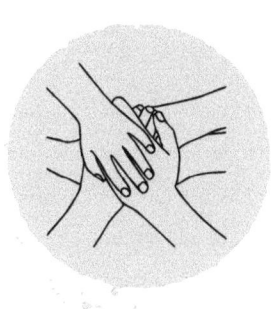

When Things Don't Go Your Way

I'm sorry things didn't go as planned when/with:

_____

_____

_____

_____

This is how you handled it:

_____

_____

_____

_____

The lesson learned:

_____

_____

_____

_____

I am proud of the way you...

_____

_____

_____

_____

The Value in Failure

Failure is a normal part of growing. This is a moment when I failed and how I recovered:

_____

_____

_____

_____

_____

_____

_____

_____

_____

_____

This is a moment where you felt like you failed:

_____

_____

_____

_____

_____

_____

_____

_____

_____

_____

This is how you handled it:

_____

_____

_____

_____

_____

_____

The lesson learned:

_____

_____

_____

_____

_____

_____

I am proud of the way you...

_____

_____

_____

_____

_____

_____

Coping With Loss

When we experience deep grief in losing something or someone, it is proof of great love.

This is the toughest loss I have experienced and how I managed my grief:

_____

_____

_____

_____

Grief is a natural response to loss. I hated seeing you grieve the loss of:

_____

_____

_____

_____

How you coped:

_____

_____

_____

_____

I am proud of the way you...

_____

_____

_____

_____

Dealing With Bad Choices

Every choice has a consequence. When it is a bad choice we can learn from it. This is a bad choice I made at your age and the important lesson learned from it:

_____

_____

_____

_____

_____

This is a bad choice you've made, the consequence you paid, and the lesson you learned from it:

The choice:

_____

_____

_____

_____

_____

The consequence:

_____

_____

_____

_____

_____

The lesson learned:

_____

_____

_____

_____

_____

_____

_____

_____

_____

_____

_____

_____

I am proud of the way you...

_____

_____

_____

_____

_____

_____

_____

_____

_____

_____

_____

Rejections and Setbacks

This is a rejection or setback that I experienced and how I handled it:

_____

_____

_____

_____

_____

_____

I see you deal with rejections and setbacks in this way:

_____

_____

_____

_____

_____

_____

I am proud of the way you...

_____

_____

_____

_____

_____

Strategies for Managing Stress and Anxiety

This is what stresses me out the most and how I manage my stress:

_____

_____

_____

_____

_____

_____

I see you manage your stress in this way:

_____

_____

_____

_____

_____

_____

I am proud of the way you...

_____

_____

_____

_____

_____

_____

More thoughts on pain, panic, and pressure:

_____

_____

_____

_____

_____

_____

_____

_____

_____

_____

_____

_____

_____

_____

_____

_____

_____

_____

_____

_____

_____

_____

_____

_____

_____

_____

_____

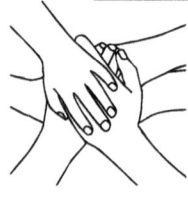

CHAPTER 9

GRATITUDE, HAPPINESS, AND LAUGHTER

Gratitude

This is why gratitude is so important:

_____

_____

_____

_____

_____

_____

These are things or people we tend to take for granted:

_____

_____

_____

_____

_____

_____

I can tell you are grateful for these things:

_____

_____

_____

_____

_____

_____

I am grateful for:

_____

_____

_____

_____

_____

_____

_____

_____

_____

_____

This is the most crucial way to show gratitude:

_____

_____

_____

_____

_____

_____

_____

_____

_____

_____

_____

Happiness

The key to happiness is:

_____

_____

_____

_____

My happiest memory of you so far is:

_____

_____

_____

_____

I shed tears of joy when you:

_____

_____

_____

_____

The time of your life that you seemed the happiest was:

_____

_____

_____

_____

These are the simple things in life that bring me happiness:

_____

_____

_____

_____

This is my happy place and why:

_____

_____

_____

_____

This is your happy place and why:

_____

_____

_____

_____

The person who always brings joy and happiness when they are around
is _____. This is how they bring joy into your life:

_____

_____

_____

_____

Laughter

This is a time/situation where laughter was like medicine:

_____

_____

_____

_____

_____

_____

_____

_____

_____

_____

We laughed so hard when:

_____

_____

_____

_____

_____

_____

_____

_____

_____

_____

CHAPTER 10

COMPARING DECADES

YOU: Class of _____   **ME**: Class of _____

▼   ▼

Fashion:

_____   _____
_____   _____
_____   _____
_____   _____

Hairstyles:

_____   _____
_____   _____
_____   _____
_____   _____

Cars:

_____   _____
_____   _____
_____   _____
_____   _____

Music:

_____   _____
_____   _____
_____   _____
_____   _____

YOU: Class of _____   **ME**: Class of _____

▼   ▼

Movies:

_____   _____

_____   _____

_____   _____

_____   _____

Books:

_____   _____

_____   _____

_____   _____

_____   _____

Food/drinks:

_____   _____

_____   _____

_____   _____

_____   _____

Phones and technology:

_____   _____

_____   _____

_____   _____

_____   _____

If we were stranded on a deserted island...

What you would do:

What I would do:

_____   _____
_____   _____
_____   _____
_____   _____
_____   _____
_____   _____
_____   _____
_____   _____
_____   _____
_____   _____
_____   _____
_____   _____
_____   _____
_____   _____
_____   _____
_____   _____
_____   _____
_____   _____

Historically significant events that I experienced at your age:

_____

_____

_____

_____

_____

_____

_____

_____

_____

_____

_____

Historically significant events that you have lived to see:

_____

_____

_____

_____

_____

_____

_____

_____

_____

_____

_____

CHAPTER 11

ALL THE LASTS
AND HIGHLIGHTS

The Lasts (last first day, packed lunch, football game, etc.)

The last _____

_____

_____

_____

_____

The last _____

_____

_____

_____

_____

The last _____

_____

_____

_____

_____

The last _____

_____

_____

_____

_____

The last _____

_____

_____

_____

_____

The last _____

_____

_____

_____

_____

The last _____

_____

_____

_____

_____

The last _____

_____

_____

_____

_____

Highlights (homecoming, prom, graduation, etc.)

Highlight: _____

_____

_____

_____

_____

Highlight: _____

_____

_____

_____

_____

Highlight: _____

_____

_____

_____

_____

Highlight: _____

_____

_____

_____

_____

Highlight: _____

_____

_____

_____

_____

Highlight: _____

_____

_____

_____

_____

Highlight: _____

_____

_____

_____

_____

Highlight: _____

_____

_____

_____

_____

Extra space for more lasts, special occasions, awards, and achievements.

_____

_____

_____

_____

_____

_____

_____

_____

_____

_____

_____

_____

_____

_____

_____

_____

_____

_____

_____

_____

_____

_____

_____

_____

CHAPTER 12

END OF THE
YEAR REVIEW

This is how we both have grown through the years:

Me:

_____

_____

_____

_____

You:

_____

_____

_____

_____

These are the most important milestones of this year:

_____

_____

_____

_____

_____

My favorite memory of your senior year:

_____

_____

_____

_____

_____

My favorite moments we shared this year:

_____

_____

_____

_____

_____

_____

_____

_____

_____

_____

_____

I am most proud of:

_____

_____

_____

_____

_____

_____

_____

_____

_____

CHAPTER 13

INDEPENDENCE

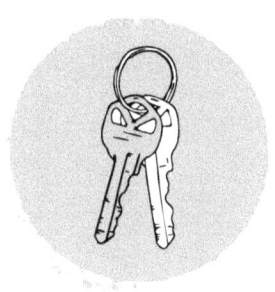

Your independence is growing. You have your eye on your future. I am responsible for letting go so you can take on everything independence requires. That's tough for both of us. I hold on, not because I don't trust you, but because I question my own success as a mom. Did I train you to handle all the responsibilities of adulting? You hold on because it sure is nice having mom's help, but also, maybe, because some of these responsibilities are tough to take on for the first time. Regardless of all the apprehension in both of us, we both must let go.

Basic Needs:

    Cooking: Grocery shopping, prepping and cooking meals
    Using small and big appliances
    Using small tools, changing out light bulbs and batteries, etc.
    Doing your laundry
    Cleaning your bedroom and bathroom
    Caring for the car: oil changes, flat tires, etc.
    Maintaining good health and hygiene
    Managing essential personal finances

Thoughts, advice, and laughs about learning these basic needs:

_____

_____

_____

_____

I am proud of how you have taken responsibility with:

_____

_____

_____

_____

This is what I remember about learning these things at your age:

_____

_____

_____

_____

Managing Your Calendar and Stress:

Waking up to your alarm and getting ready for the day
Calling for doctors/dentist appointments
Being on time for class/practice/work
Following through with plans (avoiding procrastination)

My thoughts, advice, and laughs about managing your own calendar and stress:

_____
_____
_____
_____
_____

I am so proud of the way you have taken responsibility with:

_____
_____
_____
_____
_____

This is how I managed these things at your age:

_____
_____
_____
_____
_____

Social and Emotional Upkeep:

Communicating well with family, friends, and higher-ups

Using stress-reducing techniques

Practicing gratitude

Showing empathy for others in need — volunteering

Using a cell phone with respect

Asking for help

Pulling your weight in different situations

My thoughts and advice about social and emotional upkeep:

_____

_____

_____

_____

I am so proud of the way you have taken responsibility with:

_____

_____

_____

_____

This is how I managed these things at your age:

_____

_____

_____

_____

CHAPTER 14

YOUR NEXT STEP

(College, Armed Forces, Trade And Certification Programs, Workforce)

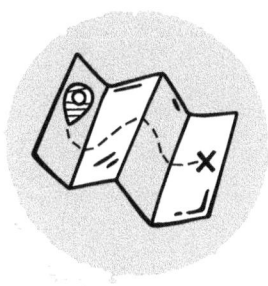

YOUR NEXT STEP

You have decided to take this next step after you graduate:

_____

_____

These are the steps you have taken to make that happen:

_____

_____

_____

_____

_____

_____

I am proud of you for:

_____

_____

_____

_____

_____

My thoughts, advice, and laughs about your next step:

_____

_____

_____

_____

_____

_____

Here's a list of things I will worry/panic about when you move on to the next phase of your life:

_____

_____

_____

_____

_____

_____

_____

Here's a list of reasons why I should NOT worry about the things I listed:

_____

_____

_____

_____

_____

_____

_____

This is what it is going to be like without you at home:

_____

_____

_____

_____

_____

_____

_____

I will still be your mom in this way:

_____

_____

_____

_____

_____

I will miss:

_____

_____

_____

_____

_____

I think you will miss these things:

_____

_____

_____

_____

_____

My hopes and dreams for you as you embark on the next phase of life:

_____

_____

_____

_____

_____

I will support you by:

_____

_____

_____

_____

_____

_____

My best advice as you transition to adulting:

_____

_____

_____

_____

_____

_____

I encourage you to:

_____

_____

_____

_____

_____

_____

MONTHLY NOTES
AND LETTERS

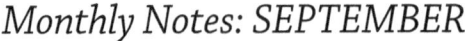

Monthly Notes: SEPTEMBER

Noteworthy things that have happened this month:

_____

_____

_____

_____

Improvements and milestones reached:

_____

_____

_____

_____

Challenges you have faced (big or small):

_____

_____

_____

_____

Special thoughts that have crept into my mind about you:

_____

_____

_____

_____

Monthly Letter: SEPTEMBER

DEAR _____,

_____

_____

_____

_____

_____

_____

_____

_____

_____

_____

_____

_____

_____

_____

_____

_____

_____

_____

_____

_____

_____

_____

_____

_____

_____

_____

_____

Monthly Notes: OCTOBER

Noteworthy things that have happened this month:

_____

_____

_____

_____

Improvements and milestones reached:

_____

_____

_____

_____

Challenges you have faced (big or small):

_____

_____

_____

_____

Special thoughts that have crept into my mind about you:

_____

_____

_____

_____

Monthly Letter: OCTOBER

DEAR _____,

_____

_____

_____

_____

_____

_____

_____

_____

_____

_____

_____

_____

_____

_____

_____

_____

_____

_____

_____

_____

_____

_____

_____

_____

_____

Monthly Notes: NOVEMBER

Noteworthy things that have happened this month:

_____

_____

_____

_____

Improvements and milestones reached:

_____

_____

_____

_____

Challenges you have faced (big or small):

_____

_____

_____

_____

Special thoughts that have crept into my mind about you:

_____

_____

_____

_____

Monthly Letter: NOVEMBER

DEAR _____,

_____

_____

_____

_____

_____

_____

_____

_____

_____

_____

_____

_____

_____

_____

_____

_____

_____

_____

_____

_____

_____

_____

_____

_____

_____

_____

Monthly Notes: DECEMBER

Noteworthy things that have happened this month:

_____

_____

_____

_____

Improvements and milestones reached:

_____

_____

_____

_____

Challenges you have faced (big or small):

_____

_____

_____

_____

Special thoughts that have crept into my mind about you:

_____

_____

_____

_____

Monthly Letter: DECEMBER

DEAR _____,

_____

_____

_____

_____

_____

_____

_____

_____

_____

_____

_____

_____

_____

_____

_____

_____

_____

_____

_____

_____

_____

_____

Monthly Notes: JANUARY

Noteworthy things that have happened this month:

_____

_____

_____

_____

Improvements and milestones reached:

_____

_____

_____

_____

Challenges you have faced (big or small):

_____

_____

_____

_____

Special thoughts that have crept into my mind about you:

_____

_____

_____

_____

Monthly Letter: JANUARY

DEAR _____,

_____

_____

_____

_____

_____

_____

_____

_____

_____

_____

_____

_____

_____

_____

_____

_____

_____

_____

_____

_____

_____

_____

_____

_____

Monthly Notes: FEBRUARY

Noteworthy things that have happened this month:

_____

_____

_____

_____

Improvements and milestones reached:

_____

_____

_____

_____

Challenges you have faced (big or small):

_____

_____

_____

_____

Special thoughts that have crept into my mind about you:

_____

_____

_____

_____

Monthly Letter: FEBRUARY

DEAR _____,

_____

_____

_____

_____

_____

_____

_____

_____

_____

_____

_____

_____

_____

_____

_____

_____

_____

_____

_____

_____

_____

_____

_____

Monthly Notes: MARCH

Noteworthy things that have happened this month:

_____

_____

_____

_____

Improvements and milestones reached:

_____

_____

_____

_____

Challenges you have faced (big or small):

_____

_____

_____

_____

Special thoughts that have crept into my mind about you:

_____

_____

_____

_____

Monthly Letter: MARCH

DEAR _____,

Monthly Notes: APRIL

Noteworthy things that have happened this month:

_____

_____

_____

_____

Improvements and milestones reached:

_____

_____

_____

_____

Challenges you have faced (big or small):

_____

_____

_____

_____

Special thoughts that have crept into my mind about you:

_____

_____

_____

_____

Monthly Letter: APRIL

DEAR _____,

_____

_____

_____

_____

_____

_____

_____

_____

_____

_____

_____

_____

_____

_____

_____

_____

_____

_____

_____

_____

_____

_____

Monthly Notes: MAY

Noteworthy things that have happened this month:

_____

_____

_____

_____

Improvements and milestones reached:

_____

_____

_____

_____

Challenges you have faced (big or small):

_____

_____

_____

_____

Special thoughts that have crept into my mind about you:

_____

_____

_____

_____

Monthly Letter: MAY

DEAR _____,

_____

_____

_____

_____

_____

_____

_____

_____

_____

_____

_____

_____

_____

_____

_____

_____

_____

_____

_____

_____

_____

_____

_____

_____

_____

_____

_____

_____

Monthly Notes: JUNE

Noteworthy things that have happened this month:

_____

_____

_____

_____

Improvements and milestones reached:

_____

_____

_____

_____

Challenges you have faced (big or small):

_____

_____

_____

_____

Special thoughts that have crept into my mind about you:

_____

_____

_____

_____

Monthly Letter: JUNE

DEAR _____,

_____

_____

_____

_____

_____

_____

_____

_____

_____

_____

_____

_____

_____

_____

_____

_____

_____

_____

_____

_____

_____

_____

_____

FINAL
SEND-OFF LETTER

Final Send-Off Letter

Date: ___/___/_____

DEAR _____,

_____

_____

_____

_____

_____

_____

_____

_____

_____

_____

_____

_____

_____

_____

_____

_____

_____

_____

_____

_____

_____

_____

FINAL SEND-OFF LETTER

_____

_____

_____

_____

_____

_____

_____

_____

_____

_____

_____

_____

_____

_____

_____

_____

_____

_____

_____

_____

_____

_____

_____

_____

_____

_____

_____

_____

_____

DATE COMPLETED ___ / ___ / _____

ABOUT THE AUTHOR

Cindy Manko, author, life coach, and host of the *Listen-Love-Launch* podcast, cares about moms. Her genuine care for the well-being of mothers and her commitment to fostering connection make her a trusted guide for those seeking direction in the ever-evolving journey of motherhood. She draws from her own journey as a parent and hours of research to empower moms through life's transitions. Cindy lives with her husband, Steve, north of Detroit where they have spent over two decades raising their three children, who have successfully flown the nest. Their six-pound Yorkie named Oliver currently rules the nest.

Cindy MANKO

www.cindymanko.com

THE JOURNAL PROJECT: *My Senior Year Through Mom's Eyes*
is more than just a journal; it is a testament to the love, support, and unwavering dedication you have for your child. It is a place to share your experiences, hopes, and dreams with your soon-to-be-adult child throughout the senior year.

You'll find thoughtfully crafted prompts with space for personal anecdotes, heartfelt letters, and meaningful advice. This journal will become a timeless treasure, encapsulating your affection and guidance.

You will:
- Document their achievements, celebrations, and personal growth, creating a collection of memories.
- Be reminded of how far your senior has come and more easily hand over responsibility.
- Learn that you have prepared your child better than you thought and better understand your evolving role as mom.
- Build resilience in your ready-to-fly child.
- Create a keepsake that will serve as a reminder of this transition in both of your lives.

The Journal Project is a personal keepsake and a tangible expression of a mother's love. The senior year is the perfect time to share/capture the memories, the love, and the dreams you want your child to remember forever.

www.ingramcontent.com/pod-product-compliance
Lightning Source LLC
Chambersburg PA
CBHW041141120626
46547CB00020B/3073